Piano/Vocal/Guitar

EVEN MORE SONGS OF THE EIGHTIES

THE DECADE SERIES

D1319101

CONTENTS

782.42164 EV23E

Even more songs of the eighties

ISBN 0-634-06479-7

HAL•LEONARD
CORPORATION

7777 W. BLUEMOUND RD. P.O. BOX 13819 MILWAUKEE, WI 53213

Visit Hal Leonard Online at
www.halleonard.com

AGAINST THE WIND

Words and Music by
BOB SEGER

there in the dark - ness with the ra - di - o play-in' low, ___ and

I found my-self ___ fur - ther and fur - ther from my ___ home, ___ and

the se - crets that we shared, ___

I guess I lost my way. ___

the moun - tains that we moved, ___

There were oh so man - y roads. ___ I was

caught like a wild fire out of con - trol ___ till there was

liv - in' to run and run-nin' to live. ___ Nev - er

noth - in' left___ to burn___ and noth - in' left to prove.___
wor - ried a - bout pay - in', or e - ven how much I owed.___

End Instrumental

And I re - mem - ber what she___ said to
Mov - in' eight miles a min - ute for months at a
Well, those drift - er's days are___ past me

me,___ how she swore___ that it nev - er would end.___
time,___ break - in' all___ of the rules___ that would bend,___
now.___ I've got so___ much more to___ think a - bout:___

I re - mem - ber how she held__ me oh so tight,____
I be - gan to find__ my - self search - in',
dead - lines__ and com - mit - ments,

Wish I did - n't know now what I did - n't know then.
search - in' for shel - ter a - gain and a - gain.
what to leave in, what to leave out.

A - gainst the wind,__
A - gainst the wind,__
A - gainst the wind,__

we were run - nin' a - gainst__ the wind.__ We were
lit - tle some - thin' a - gainst__ the wind.__ I
I'm still run - nin' a - gainst__ the wind.__ I'm

ALONE

Words and Music by BILLY STEINBERG
and TOM KELLY

Lyrics:

I hear the tick-ing of ___ the clock; I'm ly-ing here, the room's pitch dark.
You don't know how long I ___ have want-ed to touch your lips and hold you ___ tight.

I won-der where you are ___ to-night, no an-swer on your
You don't know how long I ___ have wait-ed and I was gon-na

tel-e-phone. ___ And the night goes by so ver-y slow, ___
tell you to-night. But the se-cret ___ is still my own, ___

Original key: D♭ major. This edition has been transposed up one half-step to be more playable.

How do I get ___ you a - lone? ___

D.S. al Coda

CODA

Oh, ___ oh, oh. _____ 'Til now ___ I

al - ways got by ___ on my own, ___ I nev - er real - ly cared un - til I met you.

And now it chills me to the bone. How do I get ___ you a - lone? ___

___ How do I get ___ you a - lone? ___

Guitar solo ad lib.

THE BEST OF TIMES

Words and Music by
DENNIS DeYOUNG

Moderately slow

To-night's the night_ we'll make his - to - ry;

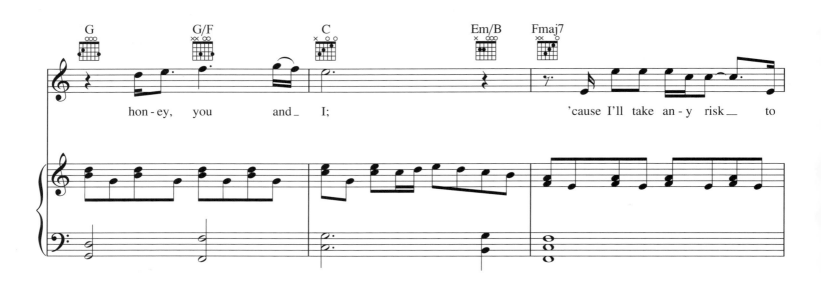

hon - ey, you and_ I; 'cause I'll take an - y risk_ to

tie back the hands_ of time,___ and stay with you here_ to -

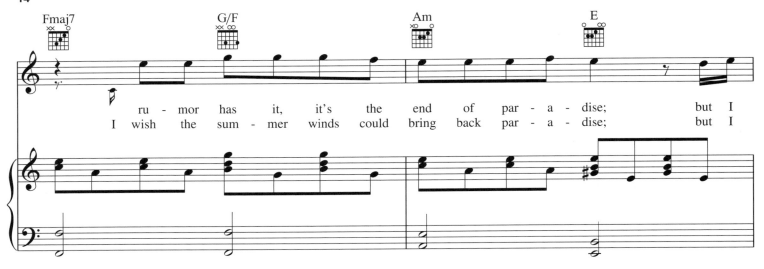

ru - mor has it, it's the end of par - a - dise; but I
I wish the sum - mer winds could bring back par - a - dise; but I

know _____ if the world just passed us by, __ ba - by, I
know _____ if the world turned up - side down, __ ba - by, I

know _____ I would - n't have __ to cry, __ no, no. __)
know _____ you'd al - ways be __ a - round, __ my, my. __)

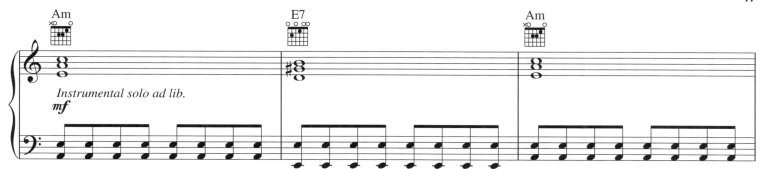

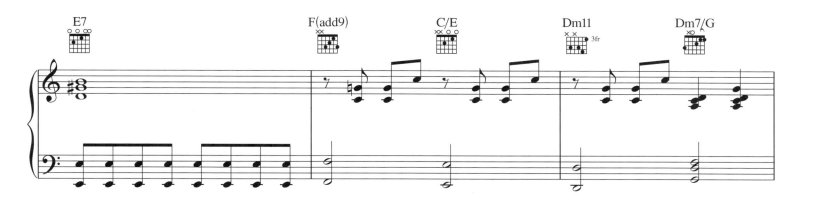

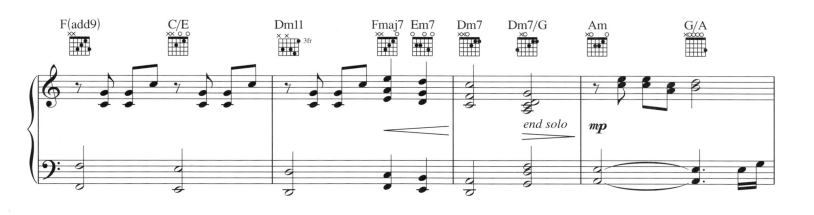

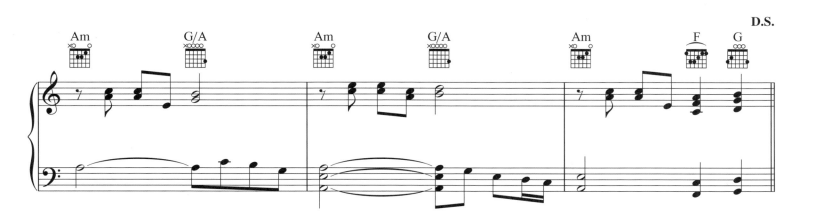

CENTERFOLD

Written by SETH JUSTMAN

Does she walk?__ Does she talk?__ Does she come com - plete?__ My
It's o - kay, __ I un - der - stand, __ this ain't no nev - er nev - er land. I

home-room, home-room an - gel al - ways pulled me from my seat.
hope that when this is - sue's gone, I'll see you when your clothes are on.

She was pure like snow-flakes; No one could ev-er stain ___ the
Take your car, yes, we will, we'll take your car and drive it. We'll

mem-o-ry of my an-gel, could ne-ver cause ___ me pain. The
take it to a mo-tel room and take 'em off ___ in pri-vate. A

years go by, I'm look-in' through ___ a girl-ie mag-a-zine, and
part of me has just been ripped, ___ the pag-es from my mind are stripped,

there's my home-room an-gel on the pag-es in be-tween. My
Ah no! I can't de-ny it. Oh yeah, I guess I got-ta buy it. My

CHARIOTS OF FIRE

from CHARIOTS OF FIRE

Music by VANGELIS

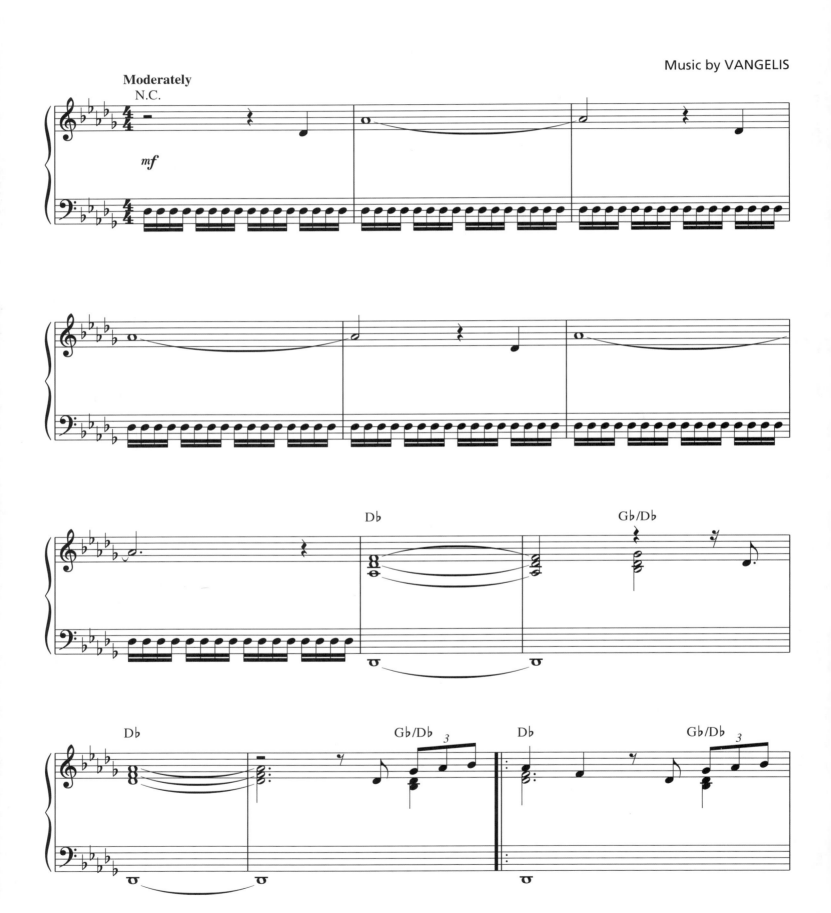

DON'T DO ME LIKE THAT

Words and Music by
TOM PETTY

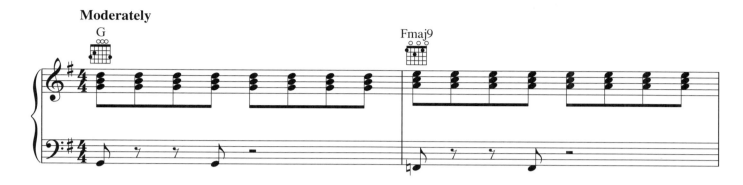

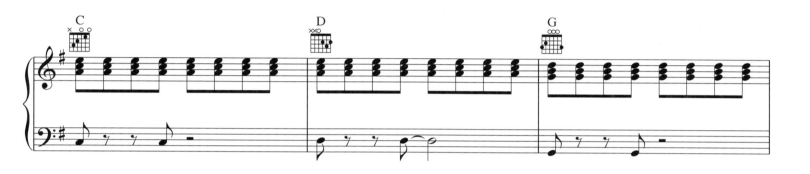

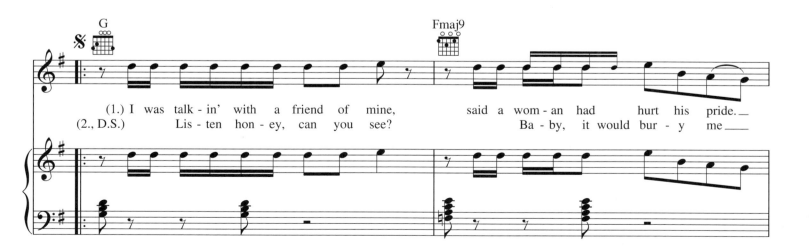

(1.) I was talk-in' with a friend of mine, said a wom-an had hurt his pride.___
(2., D.S.) Lis-ten hon-ey, can you see? Ba-by, it would bur-y me___

DON'T STAND SO CLOSE TO ME

Music and Lyrics by
STING

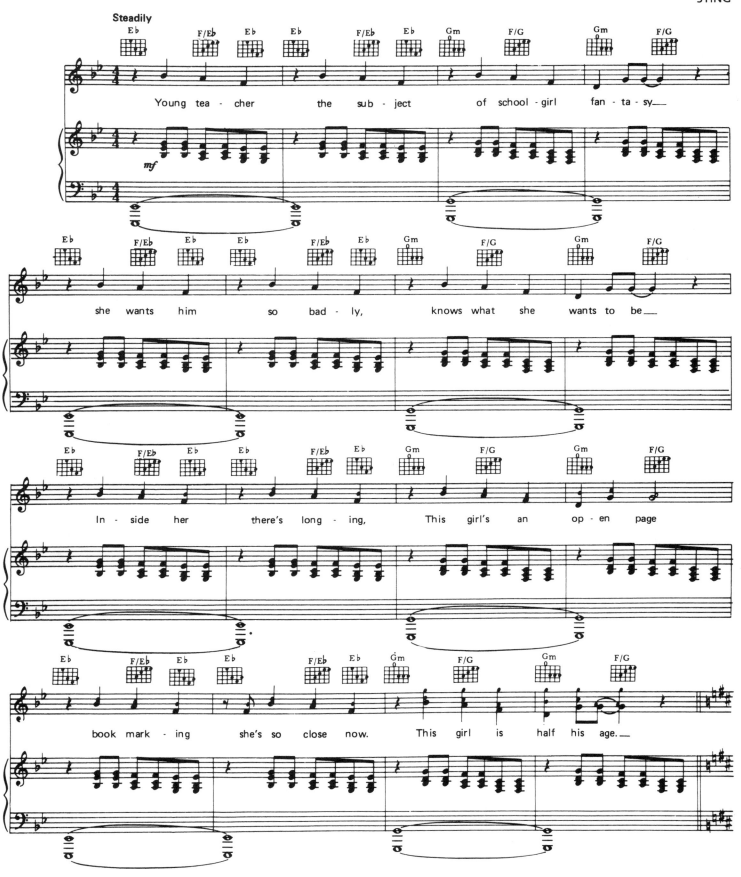

FOREVER YOUNG

Words and Music by ROD STEWART, JIM CREGAN,
KEVIN SAVIGAR and BOB DYLAN

round you when you're far____ from home.____

And may you

grow____ to be proud,____ dig - ni - fied____ and true.____
for - tune be with you, may your guid - ing light____ be strong,____
fi - n'lly fly a - way, I'll be hop - ing that I served____ you well.____

____
____ And do un - to oth - ers as
____ build a stair-way to heav - en with a
For all the wis - dom of a life - time,

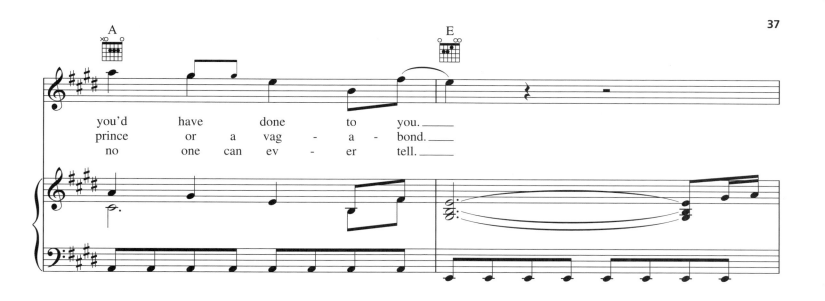

you'd   have   done   to   you. _____
prince   or   a   vag - a - bond. _____
no   one   can   ev - er   tell. _____

Be   cou - ra - geous   and ___ be   brave. ___
And   may   you   nev - er   love ___ in   vain. ___
But   what - ev - er   road ___ you   choose, ___

_____   And   in   my   heart   you'll   al - ways   stay ___
_____   And   in   my   heart   you   will _____ re - main
_____   I'm   right   be - hind   you   win _____ or   lose, ___

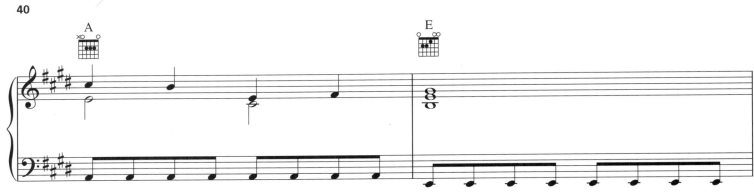

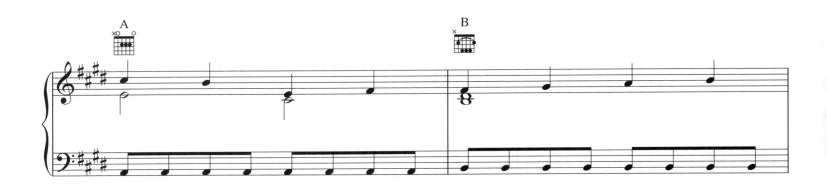

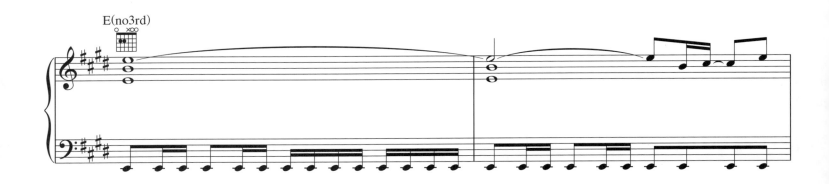

FAITHFULLY

Words and Music by
JONATHAN CAIN

GLORY OF LOVE

Theme from KARATE KID PART II

Words and Music by DAVID FOSTER,
PETER CETERA and DIANE NINI

I JUST CALLED TO SAY I LOVE YOU

Words and Music by
STEVIE WONDER

56

Additional Lyrics

3. No summer's high; no warm July;
   No harvest moon to light one tender August night.
   No autumn breeze; no falling leaves;
   Not even time for birds to fly to southern skies.

4. No Libra sun; no Halloween;
   No giving thanks to all the Christmas joy you bring.
   But what it is, though old so new
   To fill your heart like no three words could ever do.
   Chorus

HEAVEN

Words and Music by BRYAN ADAMS
and JIM VALLANCE

HIGHER LOVE

Words and Music by WILL JENNINGS
and STEVE WINWOOD

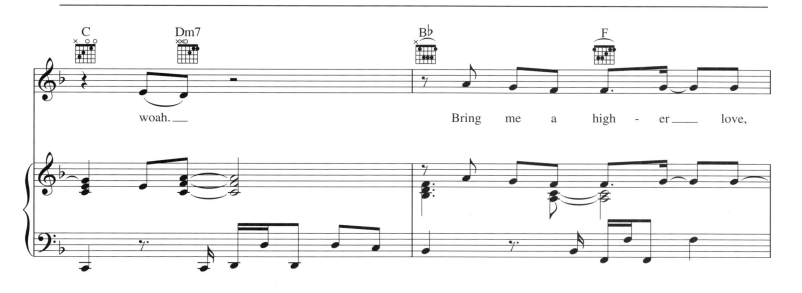

woah.___ Bring me a high - er___ love,

bring me a high - er___ love.___

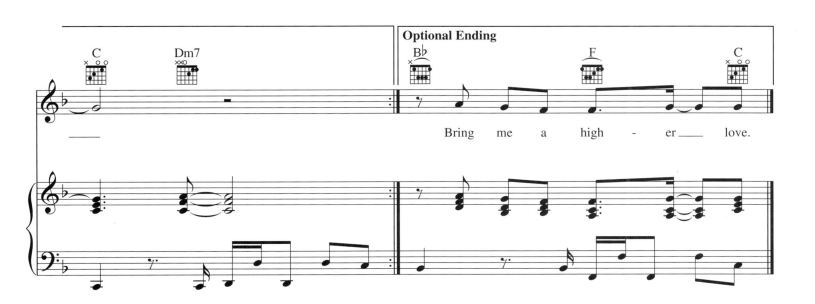

Optional Ending

___ Bring me a high - er___ love.

I LOVE A RAINY NIGHT

Words and Music by EDDIE RABBITT,
EVEN STEVENS and DAVID MALLOY

Moderately Bright

1.3. Well, I love_____ a rain - y night; I love a rain - y night. I
2.4. _____ a rain - y night; it's such a beau - ti - ful sight. I love to
5. (Instr. solo ad lib.)

love to hear the thun - der; watch the light - ning when it lights up___ the sky.___
feel the rain on my face; ____ taste the rain on___ my lips, ____

You know it makes___ me feel_____ good. ___   2. Well, I love___
in the moon - light shad - ows. ___

(end solo)

IT'S STILL ROCK AND ROLL TO ME

Words and Music by
BILLY JOEL

Moderately fast

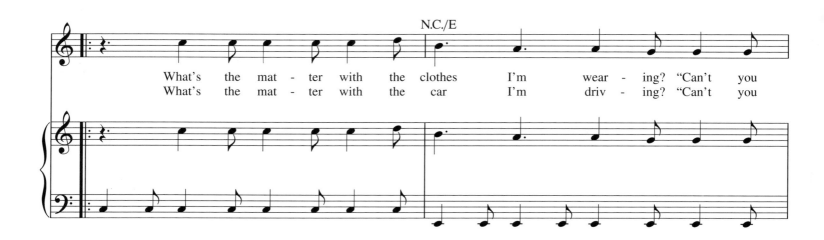

What's the mat - ter with the clothes I'm wear - ing? "Can't you
What's the mat - ter with the car I'm driv - ing? "Can't you

tell that your tie's too wide?" _____
tell that it's out of style?" _____

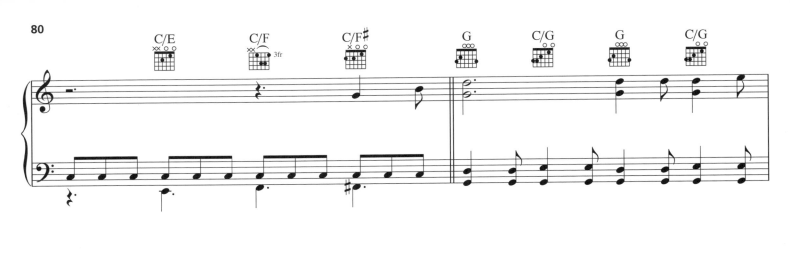

JACK AND DIANE

Words and Music by
JOHN MELLENCAMP

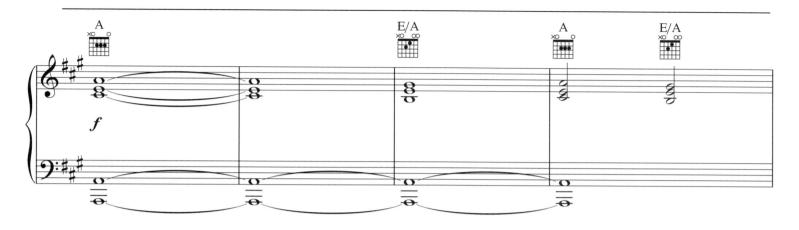

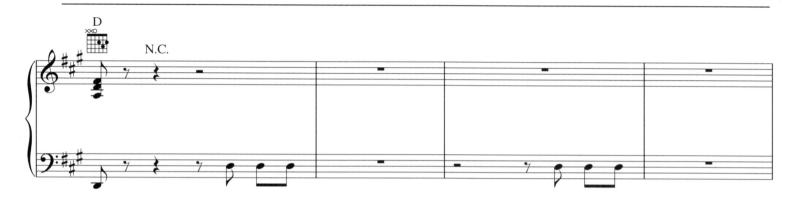

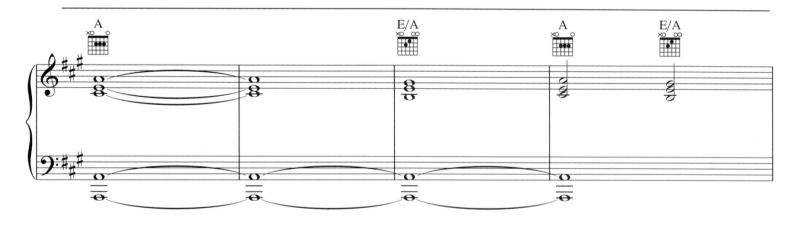

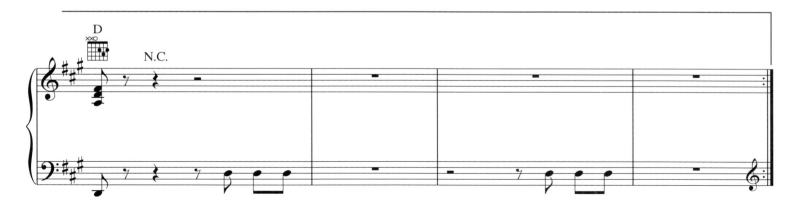

MISSING YOU

Words and Music by JOHN WAITE,
CHARLES SANFORD and MARK LEONARD

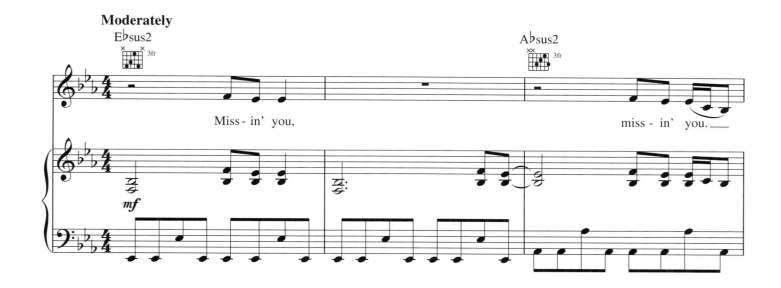

JESSE

Words and Music by CARLY SIMON
and MIKE MAINIERI

KEEP ON LOVING YOU

Words and Music by
KEVIN CRONIN

just wan-na keep on ___ lov - in' you. ___ Ba - by, I'm gon-na keep ___

___ on lov - in' you, ___ 'cause it's the on - ly thing I wan - na do. ___

___ I ___ don't wan - na sleep. I ___ just wan - na keep on ___ lov -

- in' you. ___

LADY IN RED

Words and Music by
CHRIS DeBURGH

LIKE A VIRGIN

Words and Music by BILLY STEINBERG
and TOM KELLY

NEVER GONNA LET YOU GO

Words and Music by BARRY MANN
and CYNTHIA WEIL

NOTHING'S GONNA CHANGE MY LOVE FOR YOU

Words and Music by GERRY GOFFIN
and MICHAEL MASSER

ON THE WINGS OF LOVE

Words and Music by JEFFREY OSBORNE
and PETER SCHLESS

Just smile___ for me___ and let____ the day be-gin.____
You look___ at me___ and I_____ be-gin___ to melt____

You are___ the sun-shine___ that lights my heart___ with-in.____
just like___ the snow when___ a ray of sun___ is felt.____

and I'm yours___ ex - clu - sive - ly.___ And right now___ we live___ and

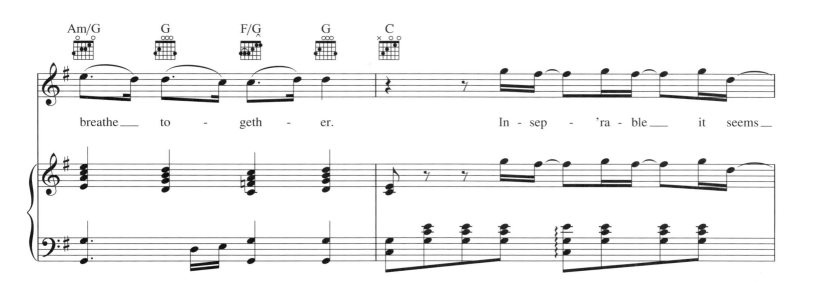

breathe___ to - geth - er. In - sep - 'ra - ble___ it seems___

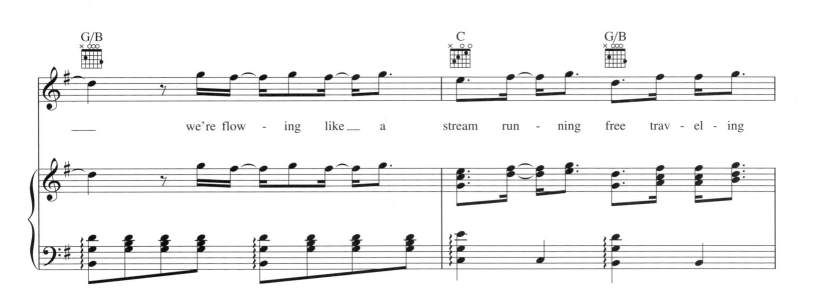

___ we're flow - ing like___ a stream run - ning free trav - el - ing

ONE MORE NIGHT

Words and Music by
PHIL COLLINS

D.S.

one more night ___ 'cause I can't ___ wait for ev - er.

CODA

Ooh ooh ooh _____

ooh ooh ooh _____ ooh ooh ooh ___

___ ooh ooh ooh _____

RUNAWAY

Words and Music by JON BON JOVI
and GEORGE KARAKOGLOU

lip-stick, plas-tic and paint;___ a touch of sa-ble in their eyes.
see you out___ on the streets;___ call___ me for a wild___ time.

(All your life,) All your life all you've asked is when's your Dad-dy gon-na
So you sit home a-lone, 'cause there's noth-ing left that

talk to you. But you were liv-in' in an-oth-er world,___
you can do. There's on-ly pic-tures hung in the shad-

___ try'n'___ to get your mes-sage through.
ows left___ there to look at you.

End instrumental

SAD SONGS
(Say So Much)

Words and Music by ELTON JOHN
and BERNIE TAUPIN

Moderately, with a blues feel

Guess there are times___ when we___ all___ need___
If some-one else is suf - fer-in'___ e - nough,

___ to share___ a lit - tle pain___
oh,___ to write___ it down___

and iron-ing out the
when ev - 'ry sin - gle

SAVING ALL MY LOVE FOR YOU

Words by GERRY GOFFIN
Music by MICHAEL MASSER

STAGES

Words and Music by BILLY F GIBBONS,
DUSTY HILL and FRANK BEARD

It's a fine time to fall __
Then you left me stand- __
Now you're left back and say __

__ in love __ with you. __
-ing all __ a - lone. __
__ you're gon - na stay. __

I __
I could-
I would-

ain't got a sin - gle thing___ to do.___
- n't e - ven get___ you on___ the phone.___
- n't have it an - y oth - er way. ___

Hap - pened be - fore I knew___ what was go - ing on.___
Were___ you just con - fused___ and did - n't know___
Tell___ me it's for real___ and let me know___

___ I ___ fell out and knew___
___ if you ___ should stay or if ___
___ why ___ does lov - in' have

THE SEARCH IS OVER

Words and Music by JAMES M. PETERIK
and FRANK SULLIVAN

SEVEN BRIDGES ROAD

Words and Music by
STEPHEN T. YOUNG

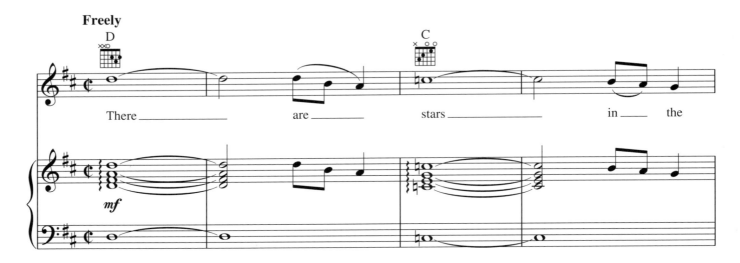

There _____ are _____ stars _____ in the

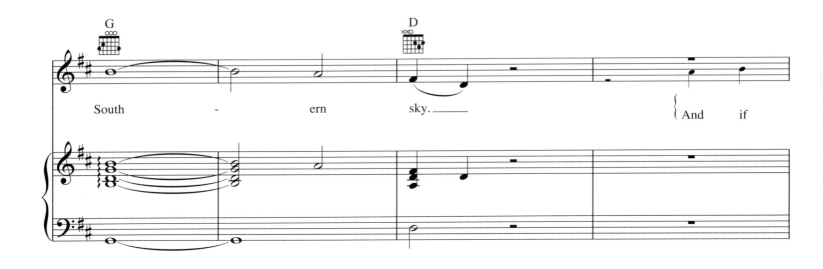

South - ern sky. _____ { And if

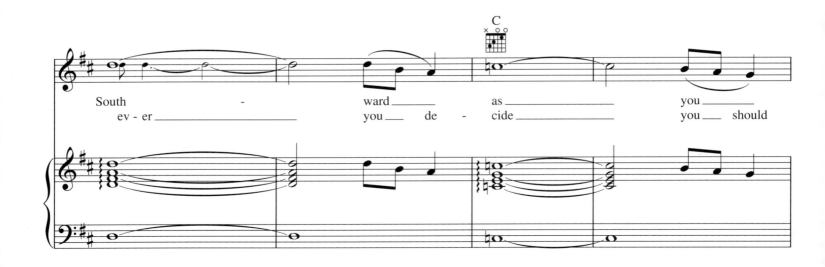

South - ward _____ as _____ you _____
ev - er _____ you ___ de - cide _____ you should

Bright Country

START ME UP

Words and Music by MICK JAGGER
and KEITH RICHARDS

STEPPIN' OUT

Words and Music by
JOE JACKSON

Original key: F♯. This edition has been transposed down one half-step to be more playable.

STRAY CAT STRUT

Words and Music by
BRIAN SETZER

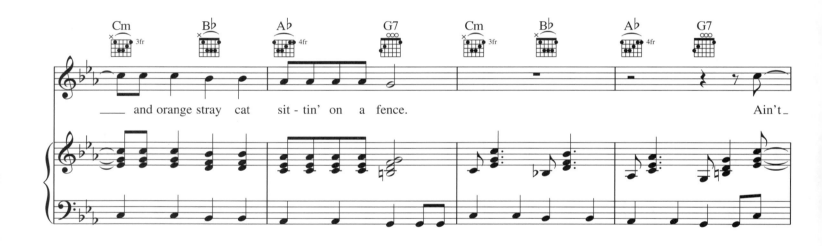

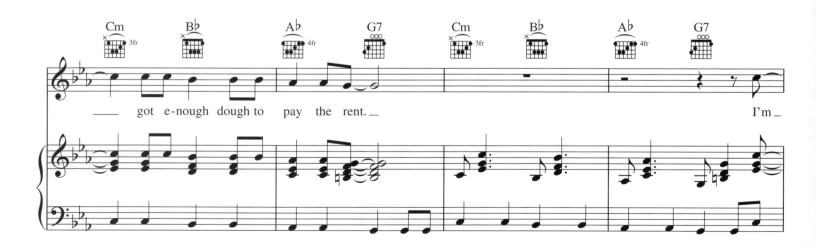

THIS COULD BE THE NIGHT

Words and Music by PAUL DEAN, MIKE RENO,
BILL WRAY and JONATHAN CAIN

We'll make it last ___ for - ev - er. This could be the night, oh, ___

___ to end all night. ___

be the night, the night to re-mem-ber. ____

We'll make it last ____ for-ev - er. This could

be the night, oh, _____ to end all

THRILLER

Words and Music by
ROD TEMPERTON

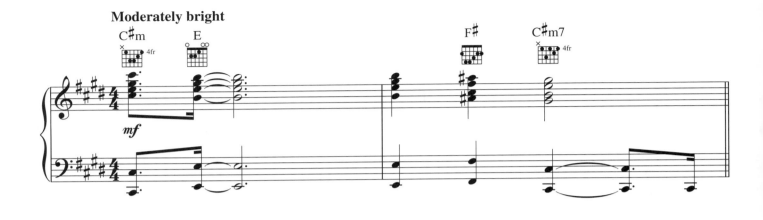

It's close to mid - night, and
You hear the door slam and
They're out to get you. There's

some - thin' e - vil's lurk - in' in the dark._____
re - al - ize there's no - where left to run._____
de - mons clos - in' in on ev - 'ry side._____

Un - der the moon - light_____ you
You feel the cold_____ hand,_____ and
They will pos - sess_____ you_____ un -

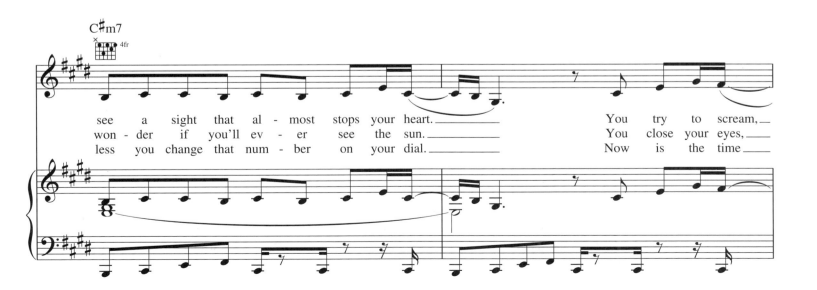

see a sight that al - most stops your heart._____ You try to scream,___
won - der if you'll ev - er see the sun._____ You close your eyes,___
less you change that num - ber on your dial._____ Now is the time___

but ter - ror takes the sound be - fore you make
and hope that this is just i - mag - i - na -
for you and I to cud - dle close to - geth -

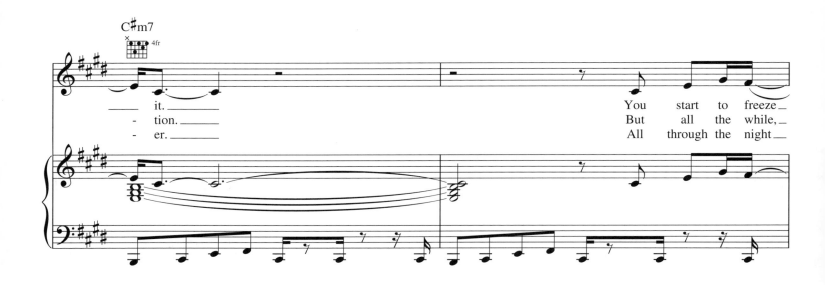

it. You start to freeze
- tion. But all the while,
- er. All through the night

as hor - ror looks you right be - tween the eyes.
you hear the crea - ture creep - in' up be - hind.
I'll save you from the ter - ror on the screen.

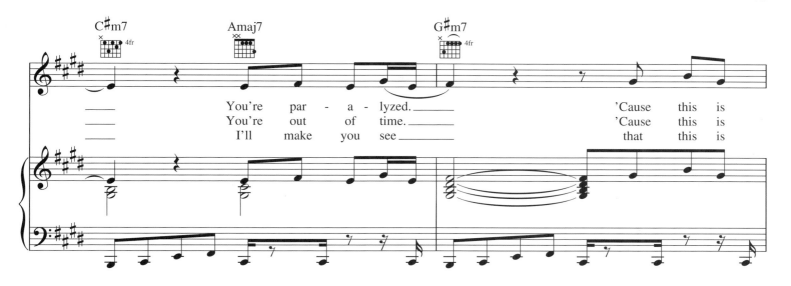

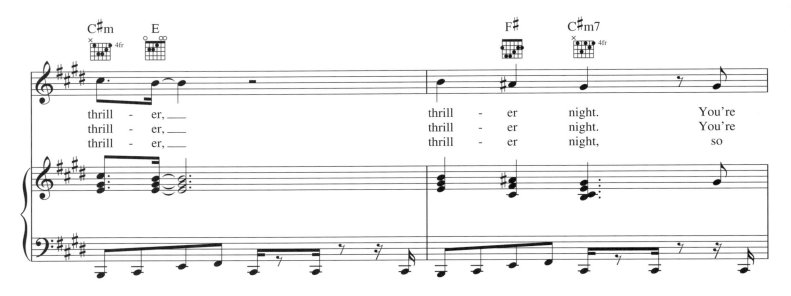

thrill - er, ___
thrill - er, ___
thrill - er, ___

thrill - er night. You're
thrill - er night. You're
thrill - er night, so

fight - ing for your life ___ in - side a kill - er thrill - er to -
fight - ing for your life ___ in - side a
let me hold you tight ___ and share a

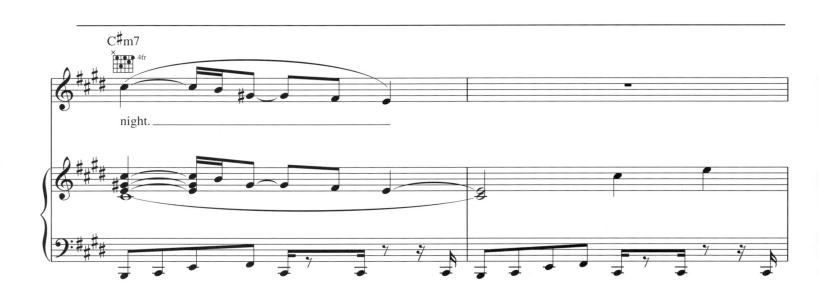

night. ___

kill - er, thrill - er.

I'm gon - na thrill you to - night. _____ 1. (See spoken lyrics)

Spoken Lyrics

1. Darkness falls across the land.
   The midnight hour is close at hand.
   Creatures crawl in search of blood
   To terrorize y'all's neighborhood.
   And whosoever shall be found
   Without the soul for getting down
   Must stand and face the hounds of hell
   And rot inside a corpse's shell.

2. The foulest stench is in the air,
   The funk of forty thousand years,
   And grizzly ghouls from every tomb
   Are closing in to seal your doom.
   And though you fight to stay alive,
   Your body starts to shiver,
   For no mere mortal can resist
   The evil of a thriller.

WALK LIKE AN EGYPTIAN

Words and Music by
LIAM STERNBERG

1. All the old paint-ings on ___ the
2. All the ba-zaar men by ___ the

3.-7. *(See additional lyrics)*

tomb, they do ___ the sand dance, don't ___ you know. If they move too
Nile, they got ___ the mon-ey on ___ a bet. Gold croc-o-

1,3,5,6

quick, (oh ___ way oh,) they're fall-ing down like a dom-i-no.
diles, (oh ___ way oh,) they snap ___ their teeth

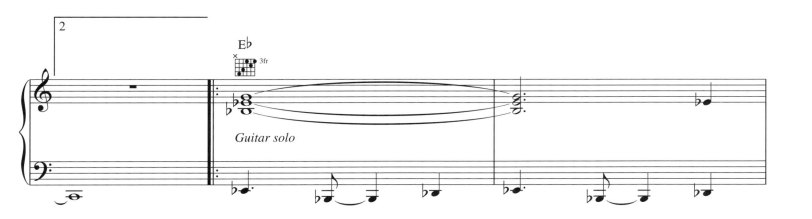

Guitar solo

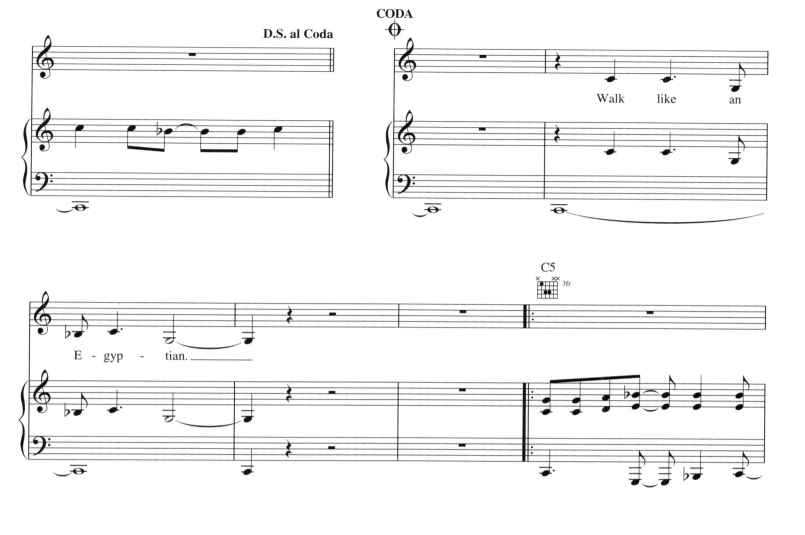

Additional Lyrics

3. The blond waitresses take their trays.
   They spin around and they cross the floor.
   They've got the moves, oh way oh.
   You drop your drink, then they bring you more.

4. All the schoolkids so sick of books,
   They like the punk and the metal band.
   Then the buzzer rings, oh way oh,
   They're walking like an Egyptian.

5. Slide your feet up the street, bend your back.
   Shift your arm, then you pull it back.
   Life's hard, you know, oh way oh,
   So strike a pose on a Cadillac.

6. If you want to find all the cops,
   They're hanging out in the donut shop.
   They sing and dance, oh way oh.
   They spin the club, cruise down the block.

7. All the Japanese with their yen,
   The party boys call the Kremlin.
   And the Chinese know, oh way oh,
   They walk the line like Egyptians.

WALK OF LIFE

Words and Music by
MARK KNOPFLER

WHEN THE CHILDREN CRY

Words and Music by MIKE TRAMP
and VITO BRATTA

Smoothly, with motion

THE DECADE SERIES

The Decade Series explores the music of the 1890s to the 1990s through each era's major events and personalities. Each volume features text and photos and over 40 of the decade's top songs, showing how music has acted as a mirror or a catalyst for current events and trends. All books are arranged for piano, voice and guitar.

Songs of the 1890's

55 songs, including: Asleep in the Deep • Hello! Ma Baby • Maple Leaf Rag • My Wild Irish Rose • The Sidewalks of New York • Stars and Stripes Forever • Ta Ra Ra Boom De Ay • When You Were Sweet Sixteen • and more.
00311655 ....$12.95

Songs of the 1900's – 1900-1909

57 favorites, including: By the Light of the Silvery Moon • Give My Regards to Broadway • Glow Worm • Meet Me in St. Louis • Take Me Out to the Ball Game • and more.
00311656 ....$12.95

Songs of the 1910's

57 classics, including: After You've Gone • Danny Boy • Let Me Call You Sweetheart • My Melancholy Baby • Oh, You Beautiful Doll • When Irish Eyes Are Smiling • You Made Me Love You (I Didn't Want to Do It) • and more.
00311657 ....$12.95

Songs of the 20's

58 songs, featuring: Ain't Misbehavin' • April Showers • Baby Face • California Here I Come • Five Foot Two, Eyes of Blue • Manhattan • The Varsity Drag • Who's Sorry Now.
00361122 ....$15.95

Songs of the 30's

61 songs, featuring: All of Me • The Continental • I'm Getting Sentimental Over You • In the Mood • The Lady Is a Tramp • Love Letters in the Sand • My Funny Valentine • Smoke Gets in Your Eyes • What a Diff'rence a Day Made.
00361123 ....$15.95

Songs of the 40's

61 songs, featuring: God Bless the Child • How High the Moon • The Last Time I Saw Paris • Moonlight in Vermont • A Nightingale Sang in Berkeley Square • Swinging On a Star • Tuxedo Junction • You'll Never Walk Alone.
00361124 ....$15.95

Songs of the 50's

59 songs, featuring: Blue Suede Shoes • Blue Velvet • Here's That Rainy Day • Love Me Tender • Misty • Rock Around the Clock • Satin Doll • Tammy • Young at Heart.
00361125 ....$15.95

Songs of the 60's

60 songs, featuring: By the Time I Get to Phoenix • California Dreamin' • Can't Help Falling in Love • Downtown • Green Green Grass of Home • Happy Together • I Want to Hold Your Hand • Love Is Blue • More • Strangers in the Night.
00361126 ....$15.95

Songs of the 70's

More than 45 songs including: Don't Cry for Me Argentina • Feelings • The First Time Ever I Saw Your Face • How Deep Is Your Love • Imagine • Let It Be • Me and Bobby McGee • Piano Man • Send in the Clowns • You Don't Bring Me Flowers • You Needed Me.
00361127 ....$15.95

Songs of the 80's

Over 40 hits, including: Candle in the Wind • Don't Worry, Be Happy • Ebony and Ivory • Every Breath You Take • Flashdance...What a Feeling • Islands in the Stream • We Built This City • What's Love Got to Do With It • more.
00490275 ....$15.95

Songs of the 90's

39 great songs, including: Achy Breaky Heart • Beautiful in My Eyes • Friends in Low Places • Have I Told You Lately • Here and Now • Losing My Religion • Save the Best for Last • Tears in Heaven • Vision of Love • and more.
00310151 ....$15.95

MORE SONGS OF THE DECADE SERIES

Due to popular demand, we are pleased to present these new collections with even more great songs from the 1920s through 1980s. Each book features beautiful piano/vocal/guitar arrangements.

More Songs of the 20's

Over 50 songs, including: Ain't We Got Fun? • Fascinating Rhythm • The Hawaiian Wedding Song • Malagueña • Nobody Knows You When You're Down and Out • Someone to Watch Over Me • Yes, Sir, That's My Baby • and more.
00311647 ....$14.95

More Songs of the 30's

Over 50 songs, including: All the Things You Are • A Fine Romance • In a Sentimental Mood • Just a Gigolo • Let's Call the Whole Thing Off • Stompin' at the Savoy • Stormy Weather • Thanks for the Memory • and more.
00311648 ....$14.95

More Songs of the 40's

Over 60 songs, including: Bali Ha'i • Be Careful, It's My Heart • The Last Time I Saw Paris • Old Devil Moon • San Antonio Rose • Some Enchanted Evening • Too Darn Hot • and more.
00311649 ....$14.95

More Songs of the 50's

56 songs, including: Charlie Brown • Do-Re-Mi • Hey, Good Lookin' • Hound Dog • I Could Have Danced All Night • Mack the Knife • Mona Lisa • My Favorite Things • (Let Me Be Your) Teddy Bear • That's Amoré • and more.
00311650 ....$14.95

More Songs of the 60's

66 songs, including: Alfie • Bonanza • Born to Be Wild • Moon River • Raindrops Keep Fallin' On My Head • Seasons in the Sun • Sweet Caroline • Tell Laura I Love Her • What the World Needs Now • Wooly Bully • and more.
00311651 ....$15.95

FOR MORE INFORMATION, SEE YOUR LOCAL MUSIC DEALER,
OR WRITE TO:

HAL•LEONARD®
CORPORATION
7777 W. BLUEMOUND RD. P.O. BOX 13819 MILWAUKEE, WI 53213

More Songs of the 70's

Over 50 songs, including: Afternoon Delight • All By Myself • American Pie • Happy Days • She Believes in Me • She's Always a Woman • Wishing You Were Here • and more.
00311652 ....$14.95

More Songs of the 80's

43 songs, including: Addicted to Love • Footloose • Girls Just Want to Have Fun • The Heat Is On • Karma Chameleon • Take My Breath Away • and more.
00311653 ....$14.95

More Songs of the 90's

More than 30 hits, including: Blue • Butterfly Kisses • Change the World • Give Me One Reason • I Don't Want to Wait • My Father's Eyes • My Heart Will Go On • more.
00310430 ....$14.95

STILL MORE SONGS OF THE DECADE SERIES

What could be better than even *more* songs from your favorite decade! These books feature piano/vocal/guitar arrangements with no duplication with *earlier volumes.*

Still More Songs of the 30's

Over 50 songs including: April in Paris • Heat Wave • It Don't Mean a Thing (If It Ain't Got That Swing) • and more.
00310027 ....$14.95

Still More Songs of the 40's

Over 50 songs including: Don't Get Around Much Anymore • If I Loved You • Sentimental Journey • and more.
00310028 ....$14.95

Still More Songs of the 50's

Over 50 songs including: Autumn Leaves • Chantilly Lace • If I Were A Bell • Luck Be A Lady • Venus • and more.
00310029 ....$14.95

Still More Songs of the 60's

Over 50 more songs, including: Duke of Earl • I'm Henry VIII, I Am • Leader of the Pack • (You Make Me Feel) Like a Natural Woman • What a Wonderful World • and more.
00311680 ....$14.95

Still More Songs of the 70's

Over 60 hits, including: Cat's in the Cradle • Nadia's Theme • The Way We Were • You've Got a Friend • and more.
00311683 ....$14.95

Still More Songs of the 80's

35 songs, including: All I Need • Jessie's Girl • Saving All My Love for You • Sweet Dreams (Are Made of This) • Up Where We Belong • and more.
00310321 ....$14.95

Still More Songs of the 90's

40 songs, including: Fields of Gold • From a Distance • Jump Jive An' Wail • Kiss Me • Mambo No. 5 • and more.
00310575 ....$15.95